The Blue Hotel

Alan Catlin

Acknowledgements

Albany Review

Art Mag

Big Scream

Bright Hill Press Anthology: The Catskills and Beyond

Chaffin Journal

Chaos of the Creative Mind

Daring Poetry

Descant

Eratica

Fearless

Footnote :Propaganda Press

Front Window

Lactuca

Lucid Star

Minotaur

Nerve Cowboy

Plainsongs

Poeming Pigeon

Poems & Plays

The Potomac Review

South Florida Poetry Review

Sub-rosa

Tin Wreath

Tulane Poetry Review

Velocities

Windless Orchard

Wooster Review

ZYX

thanks to all the editors

Cover Art by Gene McCormick

Contents

1-Mahler in New York

2-Crane Dreams

3-Wallace Stevens in Central America

1-Mahler in New York

Mahler in New York

Summer in the city, down below, trolley
cars traverse the beaten rails on airless
smoke filled nights. Travel through black
asphyxiation clouds, shocking rains
that smear generations of dirt and grime.
Heat lightning crests the Park; lost drunken
souls look up, rise, wide eyed, unsteady,
shedding their wet, news printed skins,
are lost in a sea of steam emanating from
poured concrete pavements; above them,
the maestro taps high rise apartment window
panes with his baton, moving from room
to room, dragging the metal tip of his walking
stick against iron radiator ribs, composing
the eleventh, a symphony beyond sound;
new music for the living dead.

Mahler Composing the Brooklyn Bridge

Standing on the peak of the arch,
looking down: the East River, a Viennese
orchestra in an open boat, playing
waltzes by Strauss, couples dancing,
sipping champagne, bright gas lights
visible in the distance, long after the
motions of the players have lost their
meaning and their sound; ages later,
without direction, harbor tugs in
the darkness, searchlights surveying
the fretworks, crossing the bridge,
glowing the cables, the span; illumination
after life, he who watches the river beds
change sees an elemental music, the altered
mental tides ripping everything away.

Mahler in the Underground

Pacing the concrete platform,
staring where the shifting rails
disappear into darkness, listening
as a fully accelerated express train
bursts through the station,
blurred window panels streaked
by lights flashing on and off;
a dizzy vortex of vertigo and speed.
Embarking, squeezing in with the rush
hour commuter crowd, the master
clutches the metal passenger pole,
riding west, underground, dreading
the sudden burst of blinding light
at the end of the tunnel.

The Coney Island Mahler

In the funhouse, whistling folk lieder,
lost in a private room, oblivious, avoiding
trap doors, foot activated fright mechanisms,
pressure plates, cold sudden gusts of forced
air; descending awkward walkways, composing
chiaroscuro lines, bold measured trumpet solo
parts; up against an unexpected wall, stunned,
staring through a distorting mirror; inside,
darkness visible, the fractured creative self,
outside, white water on black rock, high
ocean tides, Gravesend Bay.

Mahler in Hell's Kitchen

Trolley car tone poems: rusted wheels
abusing the rails, emerging from dense
harbor fogs and rains, milk trains
for the Hell's Kitchen run. Last stop
is the river, falling off the wharf into
the garbage with the rats; dark shadows
of bridges yet to be built, horse drawn
carriages on the cobblestoned streets,
standing up, falling down drunk in
alley ways, consumptive lungs, spitting
up blood and foam with the beer,
end of the line sounds, songs of the wayfarer
that never leave the lips.

The Resurrection

The master's face reflected in the water,
looking down, contemplating unknowable
nether worlds, disturbing a delicate balance,
subaqueous kingdoms among broken bottle glass,
the rusting gold painted caps, antediluvian
choral music in a village square, broken voices
struggling with half- tone notes, mute children
playing hide and seek, clapping their hands,
signifying the coming of the night, new
changeling moons, songs within songs;
the long, dead drunken, ancestral city fathers,
rising up, compelled by pulling inner tides
to seek the forbidden heights, their extended,
grasping fingers breaking the surface calm
of the lake.

Songs of the Earth: The Bellevue Mahler

They are gathered in a gymnasium, the mental
misfits: Mongoloid droolers, sitting, swaying
back and forth, playing with their toes, groaning
as they sway; Hydrocephalics struck dumb, puzzled
by strange overhead lights, looking up, tugging
at their hospital gowns, dilated eyes rolled
all the way inside; paranoid schizoids
hiding in corners, balling their fists, kneeling
down, moaning, howling, congregating in tight
feral packs; hysterics, weeping, crying out,
no one is permitted to touch anything, speaking
louder than a whisper triggers an endless chain
reaction of wailing; idiot savants, neurasthenics,
obsessive compulsives, basket case catatonics,
hyperkinetic psychopaths rumpling sheet music,
stumbling over gray painted folding chairs,
momentarily stunned silent by an unearthly
otherworld of music, then, the tumultuous
polytonal response in kind.

Grave Digging to Chamber Music

Mozart for the ground breaking,
formal speeches from Hamlet.
to his mentor, so many years gone,

Dies Irae sung in the original Latin
for the in memoriam, poetic verses
inscribed upon freshly honed
and polished shovel blades,
all the abandoned passions:

Mahler told he must not walk
the heights, may no longer breath
rarefied air;

six feet down and digging,
old age and creative urging are irrelevant,
what matters is excavating the music
that welds us to the world and what
we are meant to leave behind.

The Broadway Mahler

Fifty Ninth street bridge songs, exclusive
department store designer clothes, autographing
Play Bill magazines, old philharmonic
programmed texts, describing down and out
lower east side visions: *The Sorrows of
Young Werther* on stage, operatic rock, *A Man
Without Qualities* condensed to a slight three
acts, choreographed, reset in New York;
openings Off Broadway, in summer stock, all
that can be marketed will be sold; on stage,
looking down into the pit, songs of the inner
earth, liturgical jazz, heart failure visions
of streetcar conductors dressed in black,
solemn as funeral directors, open coffins,
loose manuscript pages of an unwritten
requiem mass in d.

The John F. Kennedy Airport
Transcontinental Mahler

Informally dressed, plastic earphones
plugged into elemental rock, electronic
music of the spheres, disco dervish beats;
walking an elevated, escalating staircase,
arriving inside the terminal lounge, enclosed
by chic mood music, ordering a Bloody Mary up,
watching transcontinental jets lift off into
the ionosphere, piercing barriers beyond
sound; random sonic booms level acres of
residential dwellings, commercial properties,
ears bleeding, the uncomprehending look up
considering the shattered, ruined sky.

The Titan

Mahler dreaming of a Trans-Siberian train
ride, enclosed coaches crowded with peasant
refugees smoking pipes, cigarettes, stale air.
Luggage racks overflowing with rucksacks,
suitcases, animal cages, bantam cocks tugging
wired-shut doors.
Standing up, pressed against glass, gasping for air,
outside, concrete platforms, overflowing rows
of soldiers bearing arms, clouds of mustard gas,
world war convulsion dreams.
Waking up dead, tied to the cold, unbending metal tracks,
Armageddon harpy birds circling overhead
appraising the open wounds.

The Voice that Cried in the Wilderness: The Riker's Island Mahler

Isolated, locked in, the only music is
metal cups drawn against metal bars.
Is water dripping from a leaking drain pipe,
the nightmare music sleeping inmates make
singing in dream tongues, cleft palate
song cycles. Inner Chinese boxes close
everything up tighter each night behind
bars. In the exercise yard, guard turrets
cast black moon shadows. The night watch
men take turns oiling their weapons, sighting
the all night window gazers in their high
powered infrared scopes, counting the minutes
to morning. Sixty clicks of the unloaded
rifle trigger is an hour, a year in stir,
strapped flat to the concrete, totally
enclosed by darkness. Screaming is useless,
after awhile, the presence of silence acquires
a new meaning.

The Irish Pub Mahler

Feeding dollars into the juke box,
playing drinking songs to offset the misery
of the world. Sitting, staring into heavy
smoke clouds, weary, sipping Armagnac,
inhaling the rising snifter fumes,
crossed legs stretched across the
adjacent, high-backed captain's chair.
Watching the overhead wooden fan blades
distributing the pipe smoker's aromatic
blends, the barman cutting dark stout
heads with a pearl handled knife,
topping settled pints. All the blank,
alcoholic faces reflected in tarnished
mirror rows, behind the dusty back bar
bottles, listening to their cracking
tenor voices expressing lost moments
of youth, night watch music, homesick
folk songs of an Irish wake that never ends.

The Museum of Natural History Mahler

Among the reassembled bones,
the long gone dinosaurs stalking
a primitive earth. Even opening the high
paneled windows does not diminish
dead of summer August heat,
does not diminish the oppressed,
those about to be overcome by heart
palpitations, fainting fits. See the Egyptian
mummies swathed in treated cloth,
their skeletal lips tracing hard Braille
patterns of speech on the rapidly
diminishing years. Visit rooms,
ancient pasts, holding sarcophagus lids,
early Roman villa rooms, hand carved gold
barques, amulets for transubstantiating trips
after life, stages of being contained behind glass.
Each museum floor is a ring cycle of
lost worlds, suspended time signatures,
representative man trapped below sea level,
the final exhibit, the world of the fish,
the dying blue whales rising above a fetid sea.

The Greenwich Village Mahler

Down and out on the lower east side,
touring New York after dark, winos
congregate on front porch steps exchanging
ragged brown bags, fifth bottles of Thunderbird
Port, Mad Dog Twenty Twenty, Metaxa Seven
Star.
Out on the pavement, pushers sell
angel dust, whores street walk on high
stiletto heels, children smoke unfiltered
cigarettes, exchanging stolen goods.
For an admission fee, the hallway leads
inside tempestuous opium dreams,
all the world revealed is here in the scored,
not played notes, taped on the squalid walls.

Mahler and the Man Who Fell to Earth

Sharing mental notes, communicating a
universal sadness, dreams of a desert
planet, extraterrestrial voyages beyond
stars, searching for water, for promised
lands, marooned on earth, writing music,
beaming radio transmissions beyond
known worlds:

"On my loved wedding day
all will be merry there,
but for me no joy will it bring!
I shall seek my little room
sad, dark little room.
Bitter tears shall I then weep,
  weep for my dearest love."

Unrequited love, compassion without
hope, incomplete tenth symphonies of grief,
recurrent funeral procession, drum strokes,
muffled mourning voices singing of another world.

The Lost Chamber Music of Gustav Mahler

At the Met: ornate gold fixtures, rows of
old world boxes, five tiers high, empty
plush seats, the barren stage contains the man,
deep breathing, rehearsing an orchestra
whose discordant notes echo inside these
chambered walls.

A new, unnatural dimension of life is added
to uncharted scores still locked within
the buried vault of his mind.

In his last, feverish dreams, from a crypt of silence,
music emanates, the dreaming maestro struggling
back from death, trying to create heart beats instead
of measured lines.

Mahler's One Thousand and One Nights in New York

The dead tell stories in twelve languages
stolen from the tongues of nomad tribes.

Of waking up mid-nights, in the city, feeling
the moon lighting candle wicks, stirring
hearth embers, warming fallow hearts chilled
deep inside these cold bones.

Of casting off eiderdown, a thousand chained
voices, music that freezes the lips scribed upon
window glass.

In the streets below, New Year's Eve revelers
watch the glowing orb descend, chant verses
of an Auld Ange Syne, touch the sky, are struck
silent in mid- song.

Inside, Mahler turns the family picture album page,
Marie, the love child, six years old again, no longer
dead, seems about to speak to her father of a seventh year.

2-Crane Dreams

A Study in Black and White: The Jersey Shore in Summer 1888

Outside the circus big tent, windblown multi-
colored ribbons, forced threatening-summons-
hot air music, grease painted clown faces,
great striding men on stilts juggling balls of fire,
sword swallowers and weight lifters,
gypsy fortune tellers staring at a star-gazed future.

Fireworks arc over the boardwalk, exploding
against night sky, illuminating the dunes,
beach shacks, and lean-to's of driftwood and
torn sail canvas, fishing ropes and netting.

On a sea polished board, written in a rude
hand a white washed sign says: Revival
and on another, Meeting Tonight.

Shadows in a darkened, makeshift shelter, pallid
ghost-white faces temporarily catching the gleam,
the dissipating light from above, the gathering for
the meeting has begun.

Fervent whispering is punctuated by awed voices,
some slightly intoxicated or worse.

A charismatic speaker is about to address
a small crowd of the faithful.

Explosions overhead.

Mother Crane

"I AM THE GOD OF HELLFIRE
AND I WANT TO TEACH YOU
TO BURN
BURN
BURN
BURN
FIRE----" The Crazy World of Arthur Brown

Listening, believers rock in their
pews, enthralled by The Message of the Word.

Redemption by the Jersey Shore meant
renunciation of the flesh, total abstinence
from intoxicating liquors and drugs,
a disgraced husband hounded to the grave.

The youngest of seven, an unexpected late
in life, love child, Stephen was the frail
one, wan, but exuberant of body and of mind.

He was drawn to polysyllables, a writer's trade,
like his older brother the reporter, later,
to become: the drunk, the dissolute one.

An older, favored sister, was more a mother than
his real one, died in her teens. After her death,
Stephen becomes the rebellious one,
hearing only: an inner summons.

Hearing only, 'the winged chariots of time drawing
near', those dread hymns of the four horsemen
of a personal apocalypse that already lurked inside.

The Baseball Player Stephen Crane

"I did little work at Syracuse, but
confined my abilities such as they were,
to the diamond."SC

Manny French's fastball rocked him back
on his heels but Crane refused to wear
the padded glove for catching.
Although his hands would be red from
the constant impact of the hard ball,
bruised after nine rounds of catching,
his expression never changed and his
enthusiasm for the game never waned.
Jumping up after each third strike,
although his hands were numb and his arm
weak, he would throw the ball down to
third as hard as he could. Never a strong
hitter, he was a capable one, even shrewd
in his placement, making the most of what
he had with an energy level that would
compensate for the lack of raw talent.
After every game he was the first man
at the pool hall for a beer and eight ball,
preferring, as he would later, a famous
writer, the talk of the tavern to that of
the literate man. Education, he felt, was
better learned on the ball field, attributing
his knowledge of war to what he saw on
the football field, time clearly well spent
for a man who memorialized a war he never saw.

Willa Cather's First Sighting of a Literary Man

Gaunt, hollow cheeked, unshaven
Stephen Crane, a worn volume of Poe,
as the story goes, stuffed in shabby
suit pocket, notes for a newspaper
sketch on the plight of cornhuskers
suffering the effects of a killing drought
written in neat, looping letters on his
reporter's pad. Only two years older than
the hopeful novelist, Crane seems exotic,
dissipated, and world weary in his dusty
wide brim hat leaving his lucid eyes
in shadows, his lean fingers cradling slow
burning cigarettes, a scarecrow figure
in a twilight garden, a dust bowl on
the edge of a dream. Recalled years later,
he seems almost wraithlike, nervous and
lacking assurance due to his ill health,
his eyes always staring just above yours,
looking somewhere else just beyond the horizon,
flaring unnaturally bright like suns just before
they burn out.

Stephen Crane's Red Badge of Courage

Did he, as Keats did, recognize the blood
spots welling from within as the fatal sign?
Or were the words of misplaced reassurance,
from assorted doctors, all over the globe,
enough to have faith in? Lying in a cot on
the edge of a Cuban jungle, too weak to move,
caught in the grip of a fevered dream, the sound
of thunder a kind of dread artillery, advancing
from beneath the wavering horizon of sleep,
unleashing fusillade after fusillade, bursting
holes in the clinging mosquito webs around him,
allowing the light, the insects in.

Terror stricken, reaching for the roll your-own
tobacco pouch and papers with shaking hands,
he sees himself running, heedless of what lies
ahead: dreaded shadow armies in pursuit, waving
drawn sabers that glow, a reflected glint of a
full moon lit night.

Striking a match head with the cracked edges
of a thumbnail slows the dream, the night sweats
the shivering after in the dark.

A sniper sites the red end of the cigarette,
thinking either the smoker is a suicidal madman,
quietly courting death, or a man too brave
to live.

Richard Harding Davis

"Crane jumped," Davis says in one of his accounts
of the incident, "as if he was waking from a nap
and looked at me, astonished by my voice, perhaps."
John Berryman, *Stephen Crane*

A death wish in one so young seems almost
unreal, unless you knew him, as even then,
he was courting death by covering that story
as close as possible as any reporter who hated
to ask questions but loved a gritty story, would.
Doctors cautioned him to be circumspect
with regard to his health. Was his bravado
an attempt to be struck down and killed by
a sniper's random bullet to the brain?
A bullet that could have just as easily struck him,
as anyone else. It was if he had became totally
deaf to all the threatening sounds of war around him.
Or was it simply the fists of blood cramping
his lungs, forcing him to lie down behind
the lines, while the battles raged, that made
him recover to walk the lines above the trenches
in white cotton clothes as casual and as
capricious as a moving target could be?
Davis asserts Crane was brash, a foolhardy man
of the moment, destined never to last,
meaning the writing, not the man.
Grudgingly, Davis came to admit that
no one covered the war better than Crane,
not even himself, the most admired and respected

journalist and novelist of his day, whose long
forgotten books would gradually disappear.
Except for the bound volumes on my
grandmother's shelves, that lasted long
after his long departed fame, to gather dust,
until those volumes too would disappear,
as she did, sad and old, and of no use to anyone,
not even herself.

John Berryman's Rough Rider, Stephen Crane

"Suddenly Crane, who was incapable of bravado
let himself quietly over the redoubt, lighted
a cigarette, stood for a few moments with his
arms at his sides, while the bullets hissed past
him into the mud, then as quickly climbed back
over the redoubt and strolled away. It was
impossible, H said, to question the insouciance
of this act: Crane's bearing was that of a
somnambulist.
"from J. Berryman's, *Stephen Crane*

What war was it he was seeing?
Not the Civil one unless you counted the turmoil
inside, of self against self.

He walked like a dreamer on the field of a Spanish
American battlefield, but his mind was somewhere
else, among his natural kinsmen, the dead.

Despite the clinical bill of health, the Saranac
doctor's assurance that all would be well,
there could be no doubt, he knew this was
the end, so why not find it here, on a field of
honor, among men who had come to die?

A chosen death at the hands of another might
be the way to a kind of honor, of glory,
he might not otherwise find.

Much easier to walk among the murderer's bullets,
the cannonading shells, explosive shrapnel casings,
completely oblivious and unafraid, than it was
to avoid the inevitability of what waits inside.

A Maggie of the Streets

"The ship be sinkin' but the sky's the limit."
"You live. You learn. You die. And then you
forget it all." Michael Ray Richardson

He was the kind of guy
who showed up for work
as a cook in a downtown
pub in yesterday's whites,
unshaven, not showered
slugging the last of his
Cuervo Gold pint like
mouthwash, red eyes
ready to glare at
the lunch dupes spindled
along the line.
If pressured to facilitate,
his disclaiming line is,
"I don't really need
this job, you know,
my woman works.
She's making good money.
She's a hooker in
Schenectady."
After lunch he gets a
half pitcher of draft beer,
swallows two thirds in
long, greedy gulps,
pours the rest over
his head."I really
needed that."He says.

The Hotel de Dream

'Tell me why, behind thee
I see always the shades of another love?'
Stephen Crane

Whether it be along the alleyways of jazz
clubs in the Big Easy or the streets
of Jacksonville;
Whether it be in a room fanned by wooden
blades overhead or a breeze from the Gulf
over the wrought iron railing of a veranda
through louvered shutter doors;
Whether it be on the twin posted, canopied
perfumed bed or, in a canvas, sweat soaked cot,
among palm trees and a thin gauze of mosquito net;
Whether it be on a paddlewheel boat steaming
the Mississippi, or an open one, coming ashore,
shipwrecked among the shells and sea junk
along New Smyrna Beach;
Whether it be by the uncertain light of
a hurricane lamp or by the beacon of a lighthouse
offshore, searching the densest fog of dawn,
imagination overwrought, what I see is love,
Cora's face in twilight reflected in polished glass,
holding a hand mirror nothing can be seen clearly in,
nothing living, in this not so distant dream.

The Blue Hotel

'There will be hell to pay
when the fiddler stops.'
Closing Time, Leonard Cohen

All night you can hear the sound
of weeping from somewhere down the hall,
cards being shuffled, rhythmically,
mechanically, over and over and over
and then the dealing out, a slapping of hands,
poker chips dropped, arranged and then
the silver coins thrown casually on felt,
shot glasses tapped against whiskey bottles;
turning over, facing the stained bedroom
wall, sleep is impossible.
The fading floral patterns, cracked ceiling,
footsteps above, pacing from one corner
to the next, back and forth, back and forth,
unvarying, relentless as the spring mattress,
on the other side of thinning walls, as it moves
up and down, side to side, a sentient,
mechanical beast, a vision from the séance
in the room below, rising, embodied,
through the worn, hooked oval rug;
calling out for room service doesn't help,
there is no room service, just the endless minutes
becoming hours, between then and now,
and what could become dawn.

Our Lady of the Harbor

Give us your tired, your poor
Emma Lazarus verses inscribed on
the base of our Lady of the Harbor,
an inoculation of verbs;
Give us your Date Line cruise ships
spanning the City, a Manhattan skyline
amidst the flotilla of garbage;
Give us the faces of schoolchildren,
mothers marked for lives by scars
on their cheeks, 'so everyone will know,
your mother is a bitch,' especially you,
the child of a woman is perceived as the kind
of person who fucks over her man;
Give us the Bowery, all of the Lower
East Side, homeless drunks sleeping
in puddles of piss, blocking doorways
to businesses, soup kitchens, alms
houses, half ways, the Church of St Jude
the divine;
Give us your dime store hookers, your
junkies sharing needles, your shark skin
suit pimps with their 500 dollar a pussy-
pump daily demand, their brass knuckles,
slick backed hair;
And give us your vino primo, your brown
bagged pints, your dreams of reefer madness,
mescalito, your huddled masses yearning
to be free.

Stephen Crane Spy

"I'm a spy in the house of love
no one knows what I'm dreaming of"
Jim Morrison

After the Spanish American War, days in
the trenches, nights in fevered dreams
rapt in the arms of senoritas, mescalita,
vermiculate, turning in the shallow grave
of life;
after the open boat, the voices of the drowning,
perpetually lost at sea, wave after wave
after wave, passing by, the shriek of sea birds
circling overhead, a shipwrecked sailor's mirage
of land;
after the nights spent by candlelight writing
down to the nubs, new tales of a monster released,
brief haunted tales of an internal civil war,
of death;
after the press filing dates, urgent letters
from overseas, beseeching a return to the hearth,
ignored, gypsy whore girls caressing frail,
flaccid, all too pale flesh;
after the assignations, the assignments,
this doubling life, one face for the living,
one for the dead, time must have a stop.

Stephen Crane's Ghost Story

'With your sheet metal memories
of Cannery Row
And your magazine husband
who one day just had to go.'
      "Sad Eyed Lady of the Lowlands" Bob Dylan

After the gas lights have been extinguished,
the sawdust replenished on the barroom
floor, after the final bleeding of the taps,
the ice blocks refitted in the bar wells,
among the ashes, cigar ends, brass spittoons
spaced along the boot scuffed rail, beneath
the bar stools turned upright on the mahogany
bar top, by the empty corked bottles thrust
head down into wooden crates, by the swinging
saloon doors locked against unwelcome after
hours intrusions, reflected in the tarnished
back bar mirror, polished glasses and
quicksilver dreams, the dead are revitalized,
drinking rotgut shots with draft beer chasers,
staring straight ahead in the self possessing
quiet, feeling once again the artificial heat
reaching into the deep, all the way inside.

The Open Boat

As if the sea was fired, blackened ships
moored against concrete, continental
shelves, borderless reefs;
as if sand dunes were white caps,
lifted from cracked salt plains as
blisters are divined from long dead seas,
shed skin from snakes;
as if ships were made of burnt cork,
drift woods sun bleached and dried
pure white then launched on land,
dry docked as whales are beached;
as if fault lines on a desert floor
were fissured through hollow pointed eyes
of sandblasted skulls dream fish fly
through on the way to other worlds;
as if the sun were a mirage and
the shipwrecked sea, a chimerical harbor
bell signaling a promised land;
as if an open boat was a land raft
handcrafted by master tradesmen and
the caissons that carried the dead
from the depths to the land beyond,
could prevent a ravaged heart from sinking;
as if, now, the voyage would end in a rapture
other than of the deep, floating free at
last, self-contained by light.

Stephen Crane's Southwestern Odyssey

Cast among dunes, a visual migraine
of the desert, struck completely
colorblind, eyes useless focusing
on a solar mirage, twin suns breaking
a seamless plain, relentless.
This is the dream of walking without
maps, of patterns sewn in codes
only those with defective sight can see.
By nightfall the puzzle of the labyrinth
is solved, answers to riddles revealed.
Pariah dogs and carrion birds keep their
distance, sensing the hunted is no
longer prey.
By morning, the traveler will have
disappeared inside a cloak of shadows.
His feet leave luminescent prints that
glow as trace elements will, half lives
spanning centuries although their
destination will forever remain unclear.

Crane's First Flowers in Asphalt

"I'm not ready to face the light
I had too much to dream
last night."
Electric Prunes

Whispers from dark night
alleyways, "Hey, mister,
I got something to show
you, if you got the time,"
promises of pleasures that
no brothel could provide,
"No one think twice if
they see us, just a man
and a boy," just a man and
a boy groping in the dark,
a few blocks from the
waterfront, the sound
of harbor bells ringing
in the fog.

Flowers of Asphalt Again

"Just call me angel of the morning"
Merri lee Rush

dreams of cement
down pothole city streets, rough surfaced
trolley lines disinterred, along tarnished
rails, gasoline lit alleys, black smoke
ringing fireballs in a dead calm
summer night.
Eyelids are heavy, fluttering between hurricane
storm waves, awash on Coney beaches,
seaweed mists and bodies like medical waste
floating in bloated as the tides.
Poles of light are lightning rods for heat clouds
and gunfire, the cordite thick as dawn,
the cheap tricks on lower Manhattan walkways,
those paths of ignominy, those park benches
for hell's kitchen blow jobs and a mr. jones fix,
finding a fresh vein like gold dust or a torrero
in full costume, cape waving down street cars,
police cars, men in white coats with camisoles,
gypsy guitars, African drum beat, voodoo fetish
doll hanging from doorways, eyes pinpricks
watching the sun dissolve in big red balls that
dance on east river grease all summer long,
carving names, carving dreams into cement as
flowers in asphalt

Stephen Crane in Hell's Kitchen

"He's on his own now, he's mad."
Michael Pye, *The Drowning Room*

Leaving the crowded barroom,
smoke clinging to the haze of his mind,
his eyes the color of Cognac, skin the texture
of scored glass;
walking in search of the WC, dim memories
of a long, open, porcelain trough, a communal
grave for alcohol,
Hell's Kitchen dreams, draining into alleyways,
subways, suppurating wounds.

Opening the door of an airless room,
a confined musk of odors trapped inside:
mold, piss and shit, the excrescence of a living death,
more like an excavated tomb unsealed,
than a place of respite and relief.

Closing in, a formless darkness, unnerving,
complete, disorienting.

In the distance, a wild, mythic creature is
moving in the shadows of an unknown place,
a hunter in search of game.

Jessie Conrad's Dream of Stephen Crane

After the Christmas party,
after the hemorrhage that laid him down,
that sent H.G. Wells bicycling to town for
a doctor, for a specialist, rumored to be
nearby, that proved to be false.
After the recuperative months, the silent
months, where the family's Conrad and
Crane never met, a dream came to Mrs. Conrad:
of a stretcher carrying the body of the author,
pale as the awful moon light, pale as the white
horses that drew the ambulance/hearse,
pale as the two attendant nurses, as Cora Crane's grief,
traveling with the sick man/ body, at breakneck pace
to the Coast, to the white cliffs, where mythic
black birds flew, presaging the end.
This dream concluding just hours before arrival
of the morning post, the letter that would inform
the readers of Crane's recent plight,
their reckless flight to Dover, where the Crane's
were waiting for calmer seas to sail for a Black Forest
health cure that would never come.

Stephen Crane Reads Melville, Then Himself for Inspiration, London, Near the End

Night tears a thin fabric of skin from my love's body.
Whiteness was a whale I sought in my dreaming raising
a spear with another's hand
And plunging it deep into my seeing even as I walked
through another's state of mind.
Walking, I touch fire on her lips, hear tin pan alley
music in a cheap hotel barroom
feeling the drunken lustful laughter in the sour
morning of her breath.
I rise from our death bed to compose the fractions
of our lives.
As she hovers, a Maggie off these fetid streets of
dreams, a robe of Hell's Kitchen patterns is
being weaved to lay my body in.

It was reported I stood up in the trenches of a
Spanish American War to feel the bullets
Honing in, while others cringed in abject fear.
That was just another major fabrication of my life.

I am lying now, in state, on my wife/whore's sheets
watching the bullets focus on my chest.
Seeing her, there on the edge, in tears, I could
almost begin to regret this all too short life
of dissolution and of sin but there is no time
My chest explodes.

Stephen Crane's Ultima Thule

"Pilgrims, after all, are just tourists
on their knees." Alan Bennett

His ship, The Desolation, marooned in an
ice shelf. All hands are lost in endless nights
and false horrific dawns, wavering fields of illusion.

On land, pillars of crystal are carved as rock,
windswept, drifting snow, evanescent as desiccated
light, all stripped of primary colors, leaving
only the matter that defeats sight.

Exploration is a forced, wretched wandering
as squalling winds rip ragged cloths from their eyes,
burrowing a path inward, where the traveler's
final days are spent, abandoned and alone.

His fellow shipmates all encased in sheer,
translucent ice, caught, armed and dressed
for an arctic hunt, blue lips frozen in somnolent
speech, recumbent eyes unable to focus
like carefully polished gem stones; their lost,
hopeless, visions escaping beyond a receding
horizon, just beyond reach.

Cora Crane Author

After the death, so long denied,
after the creditors, unpaid,
the hangers on, the entourage
of fame, after the children of Harold
Frederic, also prematurely dead, could
no longer be cared for,
after the soirees, the lawn parties,
the luncheons, the indisputable fact,
nothing remained beneath the veneer
of respectability but an insurmountable
debt that could never be paid.
An original Crane Romance written,
too awful to be read, stories left
in draft, more unfinished than whole,
fragmented, set aside to be packed away
with all the rest; the last unsuccessful
marriage ending in the inevitable divorce,
the headstone bearing her dates
and the name of the one she never married
carved in stone for appearance's sake
and all times, what everyone already knew.

Crane Dreams

of a play 'the blood of the martyrs',
a tale of uncountable woe, in five acts,
with a cast of thousands, dressed in uniforms
of blue and grey, dressed in formal gowns
and suits, speaking as a Henry James characters would
of finery and intrigue, beasts in a jungle, antiseptic as hell;

crane dreams
of midnight sketches of new york, the bootlegger
prophets of wharfs, stumbling drunk in the arms
of a maggie of the streets, of extinguished gas
lights, overturned carriages, spilling booze and
blood on cobblestones haloed by a hunter's moon;

crane dreams
of the urchins that crawl in the gutter, scrambling
after coins and trinkets of the pedestrians,
dropping to their knees, outside blue faced hotels;

crane dreams
of an open boat on high seas, the drowning,
screaming above the squalling tides,
cresting the waves on a derelict wreck, cheating
death with a drawn inside straight,
one or two stud games before the final game;

crane dreams
of new orleans whores, ragtime like jazz
pianos, soprano, to be or not to be soliloquies

over the open floating graves of the newly dead,
a professional pallbearer paid to weep at
the free forming wake;

crane dreams
of the black riders, 'do not weep,
maiden for war is kind', kind to the faceless
warriors, standard bearers and bugle boys,
lynched and eviscerated, gathered for a
Walpurgisnacht feast of fools,
speaking the eloquence of grief;

crane dreams
I AM NOT A POET, inscribed rhymed lines
like no other before except maybe those french
flowers of evil he clutched to his chest, a season
in hell dreaming down a Nile river of his mind,
running guns for the poets and patriots of lost causes,
lost lives everywhere, cut short by a senseless
dying young
crane dreams

Stephen Crane's Terra Incognito

"And they're bringing out the bodies
and they're bringing them to me
saying ,'Kill them now or later?'
'Kill them now or later?'
And I say, 'Now.'"
        "Pirate Jenny," Bertolt Brecht

Lines on the map to where all things
disappear. These are the streets he walks,
reliving a Spanish American war in his dreams,
recalling a Cuban malarial fever that shakes
his ravaged body, moves the pale, unsteady hand
over unlined pages. Hour after hour he writes like this,
tales that are best forgotten or destroyed,
a *Vashti in the Dark*, a white woman raped
and abandoned by a black man, her husband
a suicide; an angel boy whore for hire
Flowers in Asphalt; novels of the unknowable,
Stephen Crane's All Hallows Eve, a day of
the dead for soldiers of misfortune, bounty
hunters and mercenaries, all on the unrecorded
plains of lost continents near and far.
After hours or, is it weeks? Of wandering in
his uncharted mind, the chiaroscuro day light
blinds, the unwritten pages burning in a slow,
small fire at his feet, a fire that he feeds,
page by immaculately hand scripted page,
until nothing he has ever dreamed here remains.

Stephen Crane Afterlife

'Day deceives but at night no one is free
from hallucinations.'
Elizabeth Smart

Drinking sleep from the hand carved cup,
the rubbed clear eyes of the dreamer,
his ragged white shirt stained
by porter, coffee, and exotic teas,
steaming, as frost melt, along a cracked,
heated surface;
Words pure and polished like porcelain
pinned to burnished lips, glossed by sleep,
teeth white as alabaster stones turned over
and over and over yet by dark, quixotic seas;
Dreams as measured drams of firelight.
reflected on a blank screen of unquiet life
in an uncertain state, half way between dusk
and dawn. The silent drumming of padded
fingers on drawn, tightened skins;
An absence of noise more frightening and surreal
than a sudden shock of sound;
Dragging tides of smoke, inhaling the weight
of sunken meadows, expelling a fog of visions
unformed as nascent wings, wax melt hardened
in puddles, as stiff as statues carved in ice for flight;
Weightless and disembodied, neither here nor there,
not anywhere, a silent gas fed light fluttering in
a senseless breeze.

Wallace Stevens, Reporter, Covers the Funeral of Stephen Crane

If he saw life clearly upon occasion
he never saw it steadily; he never saw
it whole. A sense of proportion was
missing from his equipment." Wallace Stevens

The Central Metropolitan Temple on
Seventh Avenue near Fourteenth Street
was barely one third full June 28, 1900
the day Crane was eulogized.
Most of those in attendance were the sort
the novelist drew from in his
Maggie: A Girl of the Streets: derelicts,
drunken, destitute, seeking shelter
from the heat. The minister, unknown to Crane
in life, evoked Goethe, the premature death
of Shelley, a strange relationship to Hawthorne;
as if these writers held something
in common. It would be hard to imagine,
spiritual figures less likely for a man
who reveled in the hard unevenness of life.
The choir sang 'Nearer, my God to Thee'
as the horse-drawn hearse clamored over
the cobblestone street. No person watching
was aware of who was lying inside except
those in the funeral train behind; a day
of grief, stifling heat and no time left
for tragedies in this life, real or imagined.

3-Wallace Stevens in Central America

Wallace Stevens in Central America

Spirits hide in the shadows
behind candle flames, wisps of silence
hang in spider webs.
Blank pages have a life of their own,
symbolic interlocking circles are
automatically drawn beneath
the poet's still hands.
Ghost fingers rub out memories of stone
bearing the carved words like poems,
remove the verses that speak of sacred,
ancestral rites, initiations of the unbelieving.
Extend four thousand years of pagan history
beyond the written word, into dreams,
from which the eyes of the spirit chiefs
are looking back, opening old wounds,
unlocking the foreign tourist's hotel room
doors, inhabiting their dreams.
At the dark edges of sleep, sacrificial fires
begin to burn.

Wallace Stevens in Mexico

Watching the sun set between the lips
of the volcano, ordering a Texas Prairie Fire
on the veranda of the Hotel Camino Real.
Sipping Juan Hernandez over ice: "El
Norteamericano loco, crazy," the service
people say, observing the poet, lost in time,
scribbling hieroglyphs for hours, letters
on the backs of post card packets he unfolds
accordion style on the table, building a
maze of images and words, a complete enclosed
universe of his own, the waitress penetrates,
delivering a prairie fire. He meditates,
watching as the Tabasco sauce descends
through the textured layers of tequila like
an eye droplet of blood in a saline solution,
considering the next move, the final step,
the fate of nomads trapped within the maze.

Wallace Stevens in Neuva York

After Dark, reciting *Howl* from Central Park
benches. Watching the shopping bag ladies
kneel down in the bushes to pee, listening
to metal carts laden with burlap bags containing
a lifetime of scavenged used clothes,
tin cans, cracked compact mirrors, and nicotine
stained filters. Sits watching the humped back
men in the Park, clinging to cast iron
shadows, dreaming of standing upright
in a bar, chasing straight gin with vermouth,
disregarding hansom cabs outside A Tavern on the Green.
Sits watching the slow dancing ladies meeting their
necessary Man. The skate board acrobats transforming
the night into uptown express trains beyond
the Bronx, milk train rides that end inside
stone cold, closed forever, tenement walls.

In the Demented Children Institution

Drawings by demented children cover
the square, dull laminated walls with
apparitions: with mad Madonnas that spit
out burning three wheeled chariots,
Gods of a broken earth, that pull down birds
without wings, flying in a world without air.
Elemental tremors happen in the eyes of
blunt tipped, magic marker, liquid crayon
self portraits, drawn on clear plastic bags.
All day and night, their drawing is a peeling
off of the skin, a slow erasure of the self,
a compounded fracture of light inside stone cold
eyes that see all the shock trauma units as
they draw, disassembling car wrecks, stark visions
of blood, the spinning red ambulance lights and
white canvas body bags the eldest children are
defacing, crawling through the barriers, breaking
down the walls, escaping the confining limits
of institutional art.

Wallace Stevens in Guatemala

Sipping the tequila sunrise from a tulip shaped
glass through a red and white striped straw,
eyes shaded by a cream colored panama hat,
yellow, vinyl cafe umbrellas that say,
"Galliano It's Imported Naturally."
Rows of them shielding round spray painted
four-top tables, as far as they eye can see,
nothing moves but the waiter, stifling a yawn,
the poet turning pages of *A Social History
of the Machine Gun*, his delicate fingers brushing
away fat, black flies.
In the dust thick caminos, stray dogs are being
driven mad by the heat, mantilla clad senoritas
of the mind are walking, adjusting their skirts,
showing leg for all to see.
Inside the otherwise empty cantina, a deputy sheriff
from Texas drinks mescal, remembers the mass
murders of '56 out loud, staring down the wide-eyed
red neck staring back from the mirror.
Behind the bar, beer taps are leaking onto
the mold thickened floor boards, presaging
the summer rains that sweep in from dense forests,
beating on the corrugated tin roof tops
of a town between revolutions of the sun that
knows no other season but this one.

Wallace Stevens in Brazil

Travels incognito, tracing seven sand pillars
of wisdom in his mind. Watches sea
birds circling the beach, regarding the
white sails of the four mast ships on a salt
encrusted sea. Composes endless variations
of a baroque theme by Bach.
He thinks of concerts, old New England
ladies, hair tied back inside black nets,
knitting scarves and mittens for the unborn
children, whispering of the dead that have
invaded New Haven, rising from the sea,
removing their snorkeling masks, holding
mechanically triggered spear guns,
their wet black rubber webbed feet floundering
on the sand. The dozing poet's eyes close
behind silver lenses, sun glasses, nodding
over verses from *Dancing on the Grave of
a Son of a Bitch*, feeling the point of a spear
in his spine, as he falls forward, his eyes
pressed against glass.

Wallace Stevens in Buenos Aires

Street whores walk arm in arm, holding
each other up, singing German Opera in the rain.
Are as drunk as sailors on shore leave,
tripping over hard consonants, loose cobblestones,
falling down hard in torn, night dresses,
black and blue makeup, swollen lips and
eyes. Now they are lying still in the mud,
laughing, hysterical, nothing could ever
be so hilarious as this, "Silencio por favor,
Silencio " . The night watchers plead,
turning over in their pressed bed sheets;
in the morning the whores will seem unnaturally
fat, uncommonly white, almost unreal.

Los Olvidados

Kneel down at dusk before carved images,
raising their hands above their heads pleading
for a release, a swift letting go from the
eternal torment of nights spent sleeping on
park benches, their eyes wide open, bleeding
newsprint and stars, their swollen lips painted
black and blue. Even awake, they are dreaming
of holes in the universe, of drinking India ink,
tinctured oil of wintergreen, unfiltered kerosene,
and of the blue tips of stick matches striking stone,
from the cold wide eyes of statues in the park,
creating sparks that split the tight stitches of sleep
into wounds, pedestals of weathered bronze
emanating a different kind of light.

Wallace Stevens in El Salvador

Burning rubber tires signify their
coming, full speed, down the mountain,
bumping over deep dirt road ruts.
Every time they hit one, the horn sounds
until it sticks, full blasting out of
the trees, radiator smoke clouding
the cracked windshield screen, matted
with insects, animal hair, rudderless
wipers encircled by vines. Underbrush,
small trees are caught in the sagging
bumper guards, riddled with holes,
trailing vital fluids, rear doors
swinging open and shut, blood staining
the seat covers where the black springs
poke through; the ear burning engine roar
remains long after the car is gone.

Wallace Stevens in Costa Rica

Sees all the barrio rejects that sleep on
a common ground, listen to an inner music
played on broken Spanish guitars. Watch dream
musicians inside the rotten wooden cupolas
of the mind. Long after midnight, they are
a confederacy of dunces eating stolen
soft ice cream, eating rum raisin with
a heart of Cuervo Gold. Are the blind children
playing with wooden matches, with blasting
caps, dynamite sticks, they held overhead,
fuses sparkling, setting off new moons,
Roman holiday candles that end brief days
of independence.

Wallace Stevens in Nicaragua

Penitents are carrying lamps for the Virgin.
Are clad in white robes that drag in the dirt,
faces concealed behind layers of veils.
Whisper sacred words into the charmed ears
of the devout as they assemble in the dead
of a moonless night.
All of them are blind, walking down from
the hidden peaks of the mountains,
heed an inner calling.
All of them fording streams of consciousness,
volcanic rock.
Their hands have an extra layer of skin
overlapping luminous bone.
Emulate the white skulls of the martyred saints
in the bone yard.
Down below, tilting Gravesend crosses,
fallen marble angle wings, damp family crypts,
for burial above ground.
At night sacred lamp oil forms a lake of fire.

Los Adulteros

Affairs begin quietly behind locked doors
overlooking the sea. They drink chilled glasses
of Portuguese Rose, reading from El Cid,
listen to de Falla in the afternoon, eat feta cheese
and crackers left unattended, attract mice,
fat wharf rats. Outside, in the harbor, cargo
ships unload, beggared women drag their black
clothing rags through the garbage and
the dust, overturn refuse containers, oil drums,
searching for signs, clues to riddles:

"Where does the end of married life
begin, what is the meaning of wedded bliss?"

In the cobblestoned streets, stalled, overheated cars,
and cursing drivers lean down hard on their horns.
Steam clouds envelop raised hoods, the eyes
of the lovers, locked in an illicit embrace.

The Wallace Stevens Brighton Beach Torch Song

Burned out, lost in the funhouse eyes
oversee the sagging, waterlogged pier,
the lacey puddles of dried fire hose foam,
nightmare remains of blackened, busted,
burned out wall support seams, punched out
glass window panes deformed by the heat
and melted overhead metal fixtures, dead
appliances, stick figure filaments without bulb
casings, pointing down into the still smoking ruins.
Outside, the settling rolling ocean fog; hot embers
like eyes in the night.

Wallace Stevens as the Emperor of Ice Cream

Summer transforms the City.
Hundred degree heat presses clouds
of smog down against concrete,
melts tar papered roof tops, black hot drops
of it fall on the yellowed linoleum flooring,
slide between cracked wall boards.
On the sides of tenements, fire escape rods
are hot curling irons, tightly welded growths
on the skin, stretching down the body, pointing
toward the Park, where the fat women are
jogging in sweat suits on cinder paths.
Inside, the poet is the man in the black hat
who turns up the stereo, the man who listens to
the Gotterdammerung, Brunnhilde's Funeral Music
while outside, in the Park, the lake begins to burn.

Summer Rain with Shopping Bag Lady

The old lady sits eating lime jello
in the down pouring rain. Great gaping
holes mar her stockings, below
the soiled house dress the size of a
bursting-at-the-seams, side show tent.
Her man-sized raincoat is unbuttoned
all the way down, as are her too short
sleeves, rolled into cuffs.
Wears deck shoes without laces,
their tongues ripped out, revealing
ulcerating sores.
Her arms the size of fat hams that end
in hands that hold a white plastic
plate and spoon, used for feeding
the toothless maw of a giant.
Nothing interrupts the feeding,
not even the beating rain soaking all
those who must wait for the local bus.
She is impervious to anything not food.
Does not see the taut tops of the upturned
umbrellas. The lightning striking a limb
shorn tree, does not feel the electric shocks
stunning walkers in the park. She eats,
her face a mass of dark clouds,
of death black mascara.

The Texas Tower Wallace Stevens

Feeling the goalie's anxiety at the penalty
kick, the grid markings on a field of green
sites, for a mad marine marksmen, hiding in
a Texas Tower, picking out targets:
pedestrians crossing streets, salesmen
displaying used cars, housewives caught in
the act of bending over shopping cart bags;
death strikes from above.
SWAT teams are assembled, police units
mobilized, long after the eleven o'clock news
team cameras, have been rolled away.
We can watch thin sparks of light slip from
the barrel, pointing down into the night,
gray clouds of smoke, I -beaming klieg lights
localizing the sniper, caught in a crossfire,
as bullhorn amplified helicopter voices
shout:"All's clear, all's clear, proceed in
an orderly manner!"We who are left behind,
must tie up Mr. Death's package, must stand back
against the net, distracted, out of shape, looking
for something else; the penalty kick always
comes in low, and hard, and fast and always from
the blind side.

Wallace Stevens in Florida

Another strange weeping woman is depression:
is a watermelon sugar-coated eye cup, the empty
fluted cordial. Are glasses glazed by Anisette,
by Sambuca Romano, the roasted black pits,
after the coffee and the flame, the after-dinner
dishes, left-over gritty soft boiled egg spoons.
All those days of kitchen debris locked in
with the larval insect life, the black flies,
inside the sealed dreaming eyes of adolescent
children asleep in another life, creating all
the hidden divorced women climbing out
from under the rocks, stunned by sunlight,
by all the winter coat clad men lost in tropical storms.
Are waiting for the last bus to the end of the mind,
where the fat, retired, old widows are all adjusting
their cheap, their ill-fitting wigs.

Wallace Stevens in Albany, New York

Double Shots of Old Number 7, Jack Daniels
Tennessee sipping whiskey, starts a four alarm
fire inside. No one sees the flashing lights
out on a Western Avenue of the mind, blurred
images of hook and ladder trucks, black and
white car speakers, the dispatcher's voice:
"Code One Alert. All available units must
respond." No one hears road rally race car
drivers cresting a dead man's ess curve,
coming down toward the wire, locked in a dead heat,
with a kamikaze bandit running amok among
scrambled neural circuits, keeping the unclaimed
reflexive body propped up at the corner edge
of the bar, eyeless in Gaza, two hands of nicotine
stained fingers tapping a Threnody for the Victims
of Hiroshima, an executioner's song, into the wood.